One-Liners

RAM DASS
One-Liners

A Mini-Manual for
a Spiritual Life

PIATKUS

Copyright © 2002 by Ram Dass

First published in the USA in 2002 by Bell Tower, Random House, Inc.

First published in the UK in 2002 by
Judy Piatkus (Publishers) Limited
5 Windmill Street
London W1T 2JA
e-mail: info@piatkus.co.uk

The moral right of the author has been asserted

*A catalogue record for this book is
available from the British Library*

ISBN 0 7499 2394 6

This book has been printed on paper manufactured
with respect for the environment using wood from
managed sustainable resources

Printed and bound in Great Britain by
The Bath Press, Bath, Somerset

CONTENTS

CONTENTS

VI

INTRODUCTION

This book is a kind of spiritual brandy, a distillation of the lectures I've given over the course of the past decade or so. At my lectures, I like to say that my name, Ram Dass, means "servant of God," but that "R-A-M" is also an acronym for "Rent-a-Mouth": that is, my listeners and my readers rent my mouth to tell us what all of us already know. What I say comes not from me, but from the consciousness common to all of us. And the quotes in this book are the little "aha!"

moments, the cameos that have been served up out of our collective consciousness from time to time that seem to summarize something about our human journey.

Now the danger with quotes like these is that they come to you out of context, and so they can begin to sound like some kind of Commandments handed down from on high, instead of what they're intended to be, which is a collection of little teasers, points of departure for your own reflections. I think of this book as something you might have next to the coffeepot to pick up in the morning, or as something you might tuck into your back-pack to pull out during your bus ride to work, in order to reframe the way you look at your day. There are chapter headings, so you can find a quote that touches on some particular situation you're dealing with. Or you can just flip the book open, and allow your unconscious to make the choice.

Although the quotes stand on their own, they reflect the particular metaphysical context from which I operate, and so I'd like to share a little something of that with you. I have been working on a paradigm that proposes that we, as awarenesses, inhabit three planes of consciousness. You might say that we each have three "I's." Number One "I" is on the physical and psychological plane; we'll call that the "Ego." The Ego is the administrator for the physical plane, and the experiencer of the incarnation. The second "I," Number Two, is on an astral plane, where we function as individual spiritual beings. We'll call it the "Soul." And then the third "I" is on the plane where we are realized beings; we'll just call that "Number Three." As Number Three, we are the loving, creative wisdom that is God.

Now it isn't a question of our being on one of these three planes and not on the others; we exist on all three planes, all the time. However, we usually identify with only one of them, and ignore the others. Then out of that identification comes our perception, the window through which we perceive the whole cosmos. And the view from each of the three planes gives us very different perspectives: the perspective from incarnation, the perspective from karma, and the perspective from Nothingness. The perspective from incarnation—the perspective of Ego—we know all too well. The perspective of Soul is the perspective from which we see everything as perfectly unfolding karmic law, as a pattern of cause and effect. And the perspective from Nothingness, from Number Three, is the experience of being pure Awareness, pure Being-ness.

Out of its creative *lila*, through its play, Number Three creates Number Two; it creates the Soul out of itself. The Soul is never entirely separate from Number Three, but it's somehow distinguished by a sort of net of karma, which prevents it from experiencing its identity with Number Three anymore. So then the Soul chooses a sequence of incarnations, of Number Ones, that will help it work out its karma, and eventually release it back into Number Three. That is, the Soul enters into a concatenation of experiences that will allow it to acquire wisdom, through suffering and through love. And over time, as it runs through the various story lines that gradually "neutralize" its karma, the Soul is freed to merge again with Number Three.

That's the basic paradigm I've been developing—what I call my "Three-Plane Awareness" model. And then the other part of my metaphysical equation that needs explaining is my relationship with my Guru, Neem Karoli Baba (whom we Westerners called Maharajji), and with my namesake, Hanuman ("Ram Dass" being another name for Hanuman, the Hindu monkey-god).

The Hindu pantheon includes deities that

represent all the many different ways a human heart can relate to God: as lover, as mother, as father, as friend, and so on. The monkey Hanuman represents a relationship to God through loving service. Service, as Hanuman serves, is a way of making your entire life an offering, an act of devotion. Maharajji followed the path of Hanuman, and he told me that if I wanted to become enlightened, all I needed to do was to feed people and to serve people—that is, to offer my life in service to God. And that is what I have tried my best to do.

At the heart of my relationship with Maharajji is the practice of "Guru Kripa"—the Grace of the Guru. That means that I see all the unfolding events of my life within the context of my Guru's grace. I look at each situation, and I ask myself, "Where is Maharajji taking me through this? Where is his grace in it?" Maharajji is the template for my day-to-day experiences, and I see everything that comes into my life as the expression of his grace.

So now, with all that as background, I invite you to approach these quotes in a way that makes the experience of them your own. I invite you to use them to turn back toward the shared consciousness from whence the words came. I invite you to use them to come to that place within yourself where, when you're in yours and I'm in mine, there's only one of us.

Namaste!

Ram Dass

HOW IT ALL IS

If you keep examining your mind,

you'll come to see that thoughts of

who you are and how it all is are

creating the reality you're experiencing.

Our culture has trained us to dismiss any experience that falls outside our rational, conceptual framework.

The reality we live in is selected by our conceptual definitions. You and I may be in the same *physical* space, but each of us will see it as entirely different.

Contrary to the beliefs of the philosophical materialists in our midst, Awareness doesn't reside only in the brain. Awareness resides everywhere.

All emotions are present at every

moment in their unmanifest form.

Then one of them is drawn into form

as joy, sorrow, happiness, or grief.

It's very hard to grow, because it's difficult to let go of the models of ourselves in which we've invested so heavily.

Who you think you are will always
be frightened of change. But it
doesn't make any difference to
who you truly are.

There is a larger frame to the painting than the one that bounds our life's events.

Emptiness is not really empty;
Emptiness is full of *everything*. The
"everything" just isn't manifest.

Religions are founded by what mystics say when they come back; but what the mystics say is not the same as what *happened* to them.

The Soul works through a kind of "psychic DNA," which manifests on many planes—our bodies, our personalities, our dreams—using all of it to work out the karma of the Soul.

Treat everyone you meet

like God in drag.

We're being trained through our incarnations—trained to seek love, trained to seek light, trained to see the grace in suffering.

Any attraction or aversion colors your

perception of "reality."

There is grace in your life, but you have to have faith to see it. It's a contract between God and the individual: grace on the one side, faith on the other.

Who we truly are goes beyond all polarity, including the polarity of love and hate.

Phenomena arise and dissolve in the
Emptiness; the totality includes it all.

It's perfectly safe to stand nowhere.

When we're resting in Awareness, we
see that all the forms of the universe
are really, in their essence, just one.

We're sitting under the tree of our

thinking minds, wondering why we're

not getting any sunshine!

The richness of a moment comes when it's both full and empty at the same time. The truth is, we live simultaneously in time and timelessness.

You can't buy into one half of a

polarity without getting the other half.

You want good? You've got evil.

You want pleasure? You've got pain.

That's just the way it is.

We are moving toward a light that

embraces the darkness.

What we're seeing "out there" is the

projection of where we're at—

the projection of the clingings

of our minds.

Every religion is the product of the

conceptual mind attempting to

describe the Mystery.

You and I are the force for

transformation in the world.

We are the consciousness that

will define the nature of the reality

we are moving into.

You can't bargain, but you can trust.

My goal isn't to take away your

confusion. Confusion is a fertile field

in which everything is possible.

If you think you "know," you've just

calcified again.

Creativity springs from the yearning to

be the fullness of who you are.

We ourselves are the basic instruments for transformation, those forms of the Formless that allow pure wisdom to pour forth.

We kill each other over which name to

call the Nameless.

You can *be* the universe, but you can't *know* it. You *are* the answer—but you can't know you know.

LOVE AND
DEVOTION

I look at you, and I see in you

the yearning to get back to God.

That yearning is love.

Oneness is the source of love.

Real love is the One celebrating

itself as the two.

The heart surrenders everything to the moment. The mind judges and holds back.

We've gotten lost in our Ego

and have forgotten that our Soul's

only motive is to merge with

the Beloved.

Merging with the Beloved is
dissolving the boundary between
experiencer and experience.

When the heart is open, it's easier for

the mind to be turned toward God.

A lot of renunciations that seem really difficult become incredibly easy in the presence of love.

Compassion arises out of the boundaryless nature of love.

What I can give you is a little of my

faith—my faith that there *is* a Beloved.

Devotion is a process of merging
with the Beloved; as you merge,
your individuality goes by the board,
and you don't even care.

Intense love lubricates the

path to God.

God is the place where lover and

Beloved are One.

When we see the Beloved in each

person, it's like walking through

a garden, watching flowers bloom

all around us.

Devotion is the love affair between

the Soul and God.

Bhakti is a delicious intensity of love

that takes you through the doorway,

into the knowledge of the Real.

SPIRITUAL
PRACTICE

Don't compare your path with anybody else's. Your path is unique to you. Whatever path you take, it's God calling you.

I would like my life to be a statement
of love and compassion—and where it
isn't, that's where my work lies.

Information is just bits of data.

Knowledge is putting them together.

Wisdom is transcending them.

Our task is to extricate ourselves from

living *exclusively* in the world of form.

Resting in Awareness, we transform all

the "stuff" of our lives.

The practice of karma yoga boils down to this: we serve God in order to become free, and we become free in order to serve.

Why do we keep listening to spiritual
lectures and reading spiritual books?
It seems we need to keep saying it
to ourselves, over and over again,
until finally we hear.

Don't hold back—climb into your passions! But at the same time, cultivate the Emptiness.

A feeling of aversion or attachment

toward something is your clue that

there's work to be done.

If we break our identification with our somebody-ness, we can know the world subjectively, from inside ourselves, instead of as an object.

In meditation we can watch the itch

instead of scratching it.

Our practices allow us to stand aside

from our daily lives for a moment,

and to take a God's-eye view of what

we're doing here.

The essence of the Bhakti path is to use dualism to go beyond dualism by way of the heart.

The path of the heart takes you

out of the mind.

We follow a path through the heart,
and into the Presence. When we get to
the Presence through the heart—
yum, yum, yum!

Everything in your life is there as

a vehicle for your transformation.

Use it!

A woman told me that she was a
seeker, so I asked her, "Have you ever
thought about being a *finder?*"

My life is a creative act—like a

painting, or a concerto.

In mystical traditions, it is one's own
readiness that makes experiences
exoteric or esoteric. The secret isn't
that you're not being told. The secret
is that you're not able to hear.

"Enough is enough."

That's contentment!

Our thinking minds deprive us of the
happiness that comes when we are
living fully in the moment.

We're learning to become karma yogis.
We're transforming our "in-the-
worldness" to get us high, and using
our "high-ness" to dance in the world
as divine celebration.

I see my life as an unfolding set of

opportunities to awaken.

My life is my practice.

When we're trapped in the thinking

mind, we're always one thought away

from where the action is.

If you want to be surrounded by Souls,

become identified with your Soul.

It takes one to know one!

All spiritual practices are

illusions created by illusionists

to escape illusion.

SUFFERING

Suffering is the sandpaper of our incarnation. It does its work of shaping us.

Suffering lets us see where our
attachments are—and that helps us
get free.

Until we know that we can bear
the unbearable, we're always
running scared.

I've learned to respect physical pain

as a worthy opponent for my

spiritual practices.

One of my tasks with the stroke is

to avoid getting caught in the

projections of other people's

minds about it.

Birth, death, and suffering all bring us

to the very edge of what our minds

can understand.

Suffering is part of our training

program for becoming wise.

The stroke was Maharajji's way of

getting my attention.

The shadow is the greatest teacher for how to come to the light.

For me to see the stroke as grace
required a perceptual shift—
a shift from taking the point of
view of the Ego to taking the
point of view of the Soul.

Suffering is a lesson the Soul needs in

order to get to its Beloved. Joy is too.

We've taken incarnation in a time

when it's easier for Souls to get free.

This age is called the Kali Yuga,

and it's a time when the immensity

of the suffering gives us plenty of

spiritual work to do.

I used to be afraid of things like strokes, but I've discovered that the fear of the stroke was worse than the stroke itself.

If you're seeing the "shadow,"

it's because there's something in

you that's giving it reality.

Having a stroke has given me two lives

in one incarnation.

Suffering is the crucible where

real faith is born.

Pain can be the grist for the mill;

it can become the primary focus

for our meditation.

Humor and perspective are what,

for me, take the sting out of

something like a stroke.

My doctors and nurses see me as a

stroke victim. I see them as God

coming to heal me.

AGING

Aging represents failure in our society,

so each of us looks ahead and sees

inevitable failure.

As long as we identify only with things

that change, like our bodies, we don't

have a perspective that can free us from

our anxiety about aging.

Aging gives us a chance to learn to
use the shadows as our vehicles for
awakening—and the biggest shadow
of all is death.

Aging is a stage in life that's especially

ripe for us to get free.

In aging, our minds are often

permeated by memories of the past

or worries about the future.

What gets missed is the present—

and right there in the moment is the

doorway into timelessness.

There seems to be a sequence to the aging process: at first one goes through a feeling of loss; then, if we can open to that, of new opportunities.

One source of our "elder wisdom" is that our desires don't drive us so much anymore. Desire patterns change, and then new things can emerge.

The wisdom of aging is nurtured by quietness. We slow down to savor experiences, "turning them 'round in the light."

We reap in age what we have sown,

in our values, all along the way.

This society is not "user-friendly"

for older people.

Our culture's zeal for longevity reveals

our incredible collective fear of death.

We're not a wisdom society—

we're a knowledge society;

knowledge becomes outdated very

quickly, and therefore old people

become obsolete.

Growing older means preparing for

death: that is the spiritual

understanding of aging.

I think we want to approach death with a sense of adventure, freed from the past. We can use aging to cultivate those qualities.

THE GURU

A Guru is like a doorframe through

which we see God.

Maharajji made a shambles of my intellect for a moment in order to force my mind to give up, so he could deal with me through my heart.

My faith in Maharajji means I will

enter into his world view.

A sage is one who has opened the
gifts of love and death.

Staying right at the edge of dualism and nondualism through love is the relationship with your Guru.

My relationship with Maharajji is a relationship of the heart. When you experience a love like his, there is no greater joy than serving the Beloved.

Maharajji showed me that
unconditional love is a gift one
human being can give to another.
That *is* the transmission.

Maharajji is just as available to you as he is to me; you can have him as a friend, and you can use him as a mirror for what's inside you.

MONKEY

BUSINESS

For Hanuman, each action was an opportunity to place a flower at the feet of Ram, his Beloved.

When Ram asked Hanuman,

"Who are you, monkey?"

Hanuman replied, "When I don't

know who I am, I serve you.

When I know who I am,

I *am* you."

Hanuman flew across the ocean to deliver Ram's ring to Sita, to deliver God's message to the devotee. Hanuman performed that great deed, that great act of service, in order to reassure the devotee that God had not forgotten her.

In the Ramayana, after Ram's brother
Lakshman is wounded, Hanuman
carries a whole mountain to Ram,
to bring special herbs for Lakshman's
healing. When he's acting in
God's service, nothing is too much
for Hanuman.

Maharajji said, "Jesus and Hanuman are the same. God allowed them to serve Him in their different ways."

PLANES OF
CONSCIOUSNESS

If we experience the reality of other planes of consciousness, it makes us a lot less anxious about our lives, because we have a context for them.

Identifying solely with Ego, we cut
ourselves off from our heart's
nourishment, from the feeding that
comes with being part of the universe.

It's like a game of Monopoly, except that you're all of it at once: you're the iron or the top hat on the board (the Ego) . . . you're the player (the Soul) . . . and you're the Oneness in which the board and the players and you are all an *internal* matter.

It's all real *and* it's all illusory:

that's Awareness!

Across planes of consciousness,

we have to live with the paradox

that opposite things can be

simultaneously true.

Resting in two planes of awareness

rather than just one makes us reflective

rather than reactive.

My Soul is just sitting back, watching

the melodrama of Ram Dass.

"Ram Dass" is going on ego trips, and

I'm just watching: trips, trips, trips.

Of course you're seduced by the Ego.

The Ego was *designed* to seduce you

into identifying with it!

A Soul might say, "I dropped by to play

at being an Ego . . . and lo and behold,

I *identified* with my Ego and forgot

I was a Soul!"

At the moment when there's nothing
more to lose, the Ego breaks open—
and then we see who we are behind
who we *thought* we were.

Everything changes once we identify

with being the witness to the story,

instead of the actor in it.

The Ego ages . . . the Soul evolves . . .

and to the Awareness,

nothing happened!

Pure Awareness is who I was when

I was Nobody.

We have known experientially

the spiritual planes of reality, and the

experience always comes with

the feeling, "I'm home!"

We're receiving information from all the planes of our consciousness all the time, but we don't acknowledge their existence; we treat the information as static, as noise.

When we're identified with Awareness,
we're no longer living in a world of
polarities. Everything is present at
the same time.

Coming into the plane of

Soul-awareness is coming home.

Karma is the stuff that keeps the Soul

separate from the Awareness.

Humor is the ability to see one reality

from the perspective of another.

We are in the perfect circumstances for

our Souls to learn what they designed

this whole game in order to learn.

Each incarnation is a stepping-stone

on the Soul's path to God.

Our Souls aren't vulnerable in the least—so why not define ourselves as Souls?

The point isn't to deny our Egos, but to extricate ourselves from our *exclusive* preoccupation with them.

The Ego is an exquisite instrument.

Enjoy it, use it—just don't get lost in it.

We are such graced Souls! We have

the good karma to know that we're

on this journey.

I experience each moment like baklava:

rich in this layer, and this layer, and

this layer.

There are other planes of
consciousness available to us all
the time. We each have all the
clues we need to recognize
those other planes, were we not
so busy denying them.

DEATH AND DYING

There are three questions everyone

has about death: How do we prepare

for it? What is the moment itself like?

and Is there anything afterward?

What we fear about death is the

loss of control.

The fear of death is deep in this

culture, and our job is to escape

from it.

The way we regard death is critical

to the way we experience life.

When your fear of death changes, the

way you live your life changes.

It's quite a different thing when we look at death from a plane of awareness where we're not exclusively identified with being that which dies.

Most of us are convinced that we're
Egos—the things that are stuck in
incarnations—and that's why we're
so afraid of death. When we're resting
in our Souls, death is just a chapter
closing in a book.

Science has nothing to say about consciousness, so it focuses on the brain instead, and assumes that's isomorphic with consciousness. That's why science believes that when you're dead, you're dead.

"Ram Dass, what do you want at the
moment of death?" To feel ecstasy.
To feel love for God. But I want that
before I die too!

Our immense suffering about death

has to do with our being aware of only

one level of the game.

"One to me is life and death":

when you live as if that were true,

your fear of death evaporates.

It would be optimal, at the moment of death, to be neither grabbing at what will be, nor holding on to what was.

I'd like to honor the part of me that wants to live, that cellular wisdom, and at the same time be ready to embrace the next stage.

At the moment of death you will see
what your whole life's work was
preparing you to do.

If you've connected with someone

in a moment of love, the essence of

that person is right there with you

even after their death.

When someone you love has died,
sit down, light a candle, and talk to
them. Say, "You made it through.
You're OK. Relax."

When someone we love dies, we get
so busy mourning what died that we
ignore what didn't.

Death is an adventure—perhaps the

greatest adventure of your life.

At your death, if you leave this round

carrying expectations, you'll get what

you expect; if you leave carrying no

expectations, you will get Nothing.

Nothing! Think of that!

How would I like to enter my

own death? With a feeling of:

"I don't know—but wow!

it's going to be interesting."

If you're someone who's working

in palliative care, you need to value

death as much as you value life.

You value death even though your

role as doctor, nurse, or whatever

requires that you be an instrument

for preserving life.

We call what happens after death a mystery, because what happens after death is beyond our conceptual minds.

The opportunity to be with someone

as they are dying is one of the most

powerful experiences of my life, and

one that awakens me most profoundly.

When people are dying, their game is totally up for grabs—and then there's an openness in them that is stunning.

Your uniqueness as a Soul transcends

death; your personality doesn't.

Who knows what happens after death?
All the models we have of it are only
that: models in our minds.

SERVICE AND COMPASSION

True compassion arises out of the plane

of consciousness where I *am* you.

To be free, it's not enough to have

tasted emptiness; we have to

reintegrate that, so our every act is

empty, yet is compassion itself.

You can heal my Soul if your heart is
a mirror for my Soul—and your heart
can be that mirror only if you are
resting in your own Soul.

As your identity keeps changing

inwardly, the nature of your

compassionate acts keeps

changing outwardly.

Burnout is a state of mind.

The boundaries between self and other dissolve in Awareness, and you're one with what is. Out of that comes compassionate action.

The gift you offer another person is

just your being.

SILENCE

External silence can be the doorway

to inner silence.

We're fascinated by the words—

but where we meet is in the silence

behind them.

If you rest in the silence inside, all those you meet will have their spiritual hearts resuscitated.

Words engage our minds, but in silence

we hear the Presence of God.

The stroke got me to appreciate silence

as much as I used to appreciate words.

PSYCHEDELICS

Although psychedelics *was the word we used for things like LSD and mushrooms back in the '60s, a better term for them is* entheogens— *God-manifesting substances.*

LSD is a product of science. The mind produced that which takes us beyond the mind—that's pretty good!

Medical marijuana is a plant that heals the body and heals the Soul—"healing" meaning that it helps the Soul in its travels to the One.

The reality I moved into when I took mushrooms for the first time was so deeply a part of my being that I couldn't believe I had lived my whole life having forgotten it. It wasn't something I was learning about, it was something I was *remembering*.

Entheogens have given this culture a spiritual infusion, and an openness to Eastern religions and mystical traditions.

The '60s aren't dead; fragments of
the psychedelic message are
everywhere around us—in politics,
in art, everywhere.

We see the evidence of entheogens

in the growth of compassion,

because compassion arises from the

One Awareness, out of which the

many have come.

I use medical marijuana for the
pain and spasticity associated with
my stroke. But the marijuana also
has an interesting side effect:
it gives me access to other planes
of my consciousness.

SOCIAL AWARENESS

The most interesting game is no longer

the one being played in the political

arena—it's the game of consciousness.

If you would truly bring peace to the world, identify with that place within you where you are Peace.

As one individual changes,

the system changes.

Once we're free,

our acts can free other people.

We ourselves have created the
ecological conditions that are
strangling us. Think of that:
no one has done it *to* us—we humans
have done it to ourselves.

Learning how not to be trapped in our

roles is a great spiritual art form.

To materialist eyes, India is a
developing country; to spiritual
eyes, the United States is a
developing country.

As we each listen to the intuitive

message of our hearts, the society of

which we are a part listens too.

We're seeing an accelerating change in our collective consciousness that will change the way we walk on the earth.

Let's trade in all our judging for appreciating. Let's lay down our righteousness and just *be* together.

In our relationships, how much can we allow them to become new, and how much do we cling to what they used to be yesterday?

What you meet in another being is

the projection of your own level

of evolution.

Whenever I identify with a need or a desire, everyone else becomes an object to achieve that desire.

In most of our human relationships,

we spend much of our time reassuring

one another that our costumes of

identity are on straight.

Don't take yourself so personally.

Kids need to become somebody; that's true. But ideally they should become somebody in the presence of parents who see themselves as Nobodys being somebodys.

Our interactions with one another

reflect a dance between love and fear.

We are here to remind each other

what it's all about.

A moment comes when "other"

is no longer other.

LIBERATION

Being fully present in each moment

is the doorway into another level of

consciousness; "Be Here Now"

was right!

Our journey is about being more deeply involved in life, and yet less attached to it.

Facing what *is* is the root of liberation.

We let go of knowledge to come

into the totality—and out of that

comes wisdom.

You can't be free if in any fashion

you're holding the hand of fear.

Wise beings can be peaceful in the
midst of chaos, experiencing delight
in the changing play of forms.

We can't push away the world.

We have to enter into life fully in

order to become free.

When we find the place in

ourselves that is not vulnerable—

what freedom that is!

Our whole spiritual transformation

brings us to the point where we realize

that in our own being, we are enough.

The closer we come to Realization,

the more we become instruments of

true compassion.

What is Freedom? It's Awareness not

trapped in attraction or aversion.

Freedom of Awareness: that's what

I wish for every one of us.

Tape Library

THE RAM DASS TAPE LIBRARY

Recordings of Ram Dass's talks (including those from which this book was derived) are available through the Ram Dass Tape Library Foundation, which is also the source for information about Ram Dass's schedule of lectures and workshops. Please visit the Tape Library's website, or call to request a current catalog.

Ram Dass Tape Library Foundation
524 San Anselmo Avenue, #203
San Anselmo, CA 94960
USA
www.RamDassTapes.org
Phone: 001-415-499-8587 or 001-800-248-1008